IMAGES
of America

WALTHAM

The Charles River runs through the southern district of Waltham.

IMAGES
of America

WALTHAM

Melissa Mannon

ARCADIA

Published by Arcadia Publishing,
an imprint of Tempus Publishing, Inc.
2 Cumberland Street
Charleston, SC 29401

Printed in Great Britain.

Library of Congress Catalog Card Number: 98-85876

For all general information contact Arcadia Publishing at:
Telephone 843-853-2070
Fax 843-853-0044
E-Mail arcadia@charleston.net

For customer service and orders:
Toll-Free 1-888-313-BOOK

Visit us on the internet at http://www.arcadiaimages.com

Contents

Acknowledgments

The majority of photographs in this book are from the collection of the Waltham Room at the Waltham Public Library. This collection includes over three thousand photographs and negatives. I would like to thank Library Director Tom Jewell and the Waltham Public Library reference department (Amanda, Barbara, Dave, Kate, Marialice, and Paula) for their support during the writing of this book.

I would also like to thank the other area institutions and people who loaned or donated material, including the following: Brad Bigham; the Charles River Museum of Industry; the First Evangelical Lutheran Church; the First Presbyterian Church; the Girl Scout Museum at Cedar Hill; GTE; the Robert Treat Paine Estate; Temple Beth Israel; the Waltham Evangelical Free Church; the Waltham Historical Society; and the Waltham Museum. I encourage anyone interested in further exploring Waltham history to visit the wonderful historical collections and sites in Waltham.

Finally, I give my thanks to the following individuals who offered me their support and/or expertise: Paula Cerrato; Tamara Chernow; Sheila Fitzpatrick; Debbie Johnstone; John Morrison; Wade Putnam; Pat Ross; and Kim Theriault. I also want to give special thanks to my husband, Kevin, who encouraged me to pursue this project.

Introduction

Waltham, Massachusetts, rapidly grew from a small rural town with an agrarian economy to a thriving industrial center due to its ideal location and natural resources. The city is located about 10 miles west of Boston. During the colonial era, items could be shipped to urban centers along the trade route that passed through Waltham over the Boston Post Road, which is now known as Main Street or Route 20. The Charles River, which empties into the Atlantic Ocean through Boston, also runs through Waltham in the town's southern district. The river and its tributaries provided early residents with fertile land on which they could plant crops. In the early 19th century, industrialists realized they could take advantage of the area's resources for manufacturing purposes by harnessing the power of the river.

Waltham originally was the "Middle Precinct" of Watertown and Weston was the "West Precinct." The mother town was a thriving colonial community with a town center too far away from Waltham to meet the community's religious and educational needs. Waltham separated from Watertown in 1738 to establish its own church and government. Comprising a total of approximately 9,000 acres, it is bordered by the towns of Belmont, Lexington, Lincoln, Newton, Watertown, and Weston. Waltham was popular in its early history as a summer retreat for wealthy Bostonians. Among the more famous families who built their country estates here were the Lowells, the Gores, and the Lymans. The waterways in town provided fine vistas and recreational opportunities for residents.

Waltham's first world-renowned industry was established in 1813. Founded by Francis Cabot Lowell, Nathan Appleton, and Patrick Tracy Jackson, the Boston Manufacturing Company was the first mill in the world to mass-produce cotton cloth from start to finish under one roof. The "Waltham System," which was a synthesis of forward-thinking American technological and organizational practices, was started here. The company relied heavily on young women between the ages of 18 and 25 for its workforce and was known for its beneficent treatment and paternal employment practices. The entrepreneurs at the Boston Manufacturing Company later went on to establish the town and mills of Lowell employing the progressive company methods they used in Waltham.

Waltham continued its growth as an industrial center with the arrival of the Waltham Improvement Company from Roxbury in 1854. Later renamed the Waltham Watch Company, this factory was the largest watch manufacturer in the world in the 19th century and was the source of Waltham's moniker, "Watch City." The company was the first in the world to develop techniques for the mass production of inexpensive, high-quality watches. Many Union soldiers relied on them throughout the Civil War.

Waltham's population quadrupled between 1850 and 1890 with the increased work opportunities. It soon became clear that the town needed a new form of government to accommodate its growth. On June 2, 1884, by Act of Incorporation, Waltham became a city. The New England form of town government that Waltham previously had gave voters legislative rights and gave boards of selectmen executive responsibilities. Waltham's first form of city government granted a single board of aldermen the power to make the law and administer it.

In 1929, Waltham began a third economic boom with the establishment of Raytheon Corporation and the electronics industry. Other businesses followed in the ensuing decades. Today, Waltham is home to major corporations including GTE, Polaroid Corporation, Thermo-Electron Corporation, and Parametric Technologies. Waltham and neighboring towns on the belt of Route 128 have together become one of the largest manufacturing centers in the country in the computer and electronics industries. According to the most recent census, approximately 58,000 people now live in Waltham, with an additional 43,400 people commuting to work here.

This book focuses on Waltham from the dawn of the Industrial Revolution to the birth of the Computer Age—from 1813 to 1960. Photographs have been selected from the Waltham Public Library's Waltham Room Collection and from other Waltham historical institutions. The bulk of this collection looks at the businesses and industries of Waltham, which have so dramatically influenced the direction of the city. Other images focus on the social development of the town through its churches, educational institutions, and main streets. There are photographs of many people who aided the growth of the town, the homes these people created, and their recreational activities.

One
Boston Manufacturing Company

Between 1780 and 1790, John Boies was the first to make use of the waterpower in Waltham, erecting a paper mill along the upper falls of the Charles River. Acknowledged as one of the prettiest areas in town, the site where he established his business was called "Eden Vale." Dated 1793, this printed woodcut shows the John Boies paper mill and his home. The Boston Manufacturing Company purchased the property in 1812.

The Boston Manufacturing Company was the first company in the world to produce cotton cloth from start to finish under one roof. The company erected its first mill in 1813 along the Charles River. The "Waltham System" of manufacture begun here was an innovative mix of advanced technological and organizational practices that improved on the standards of the European Industrial Revolution.

Between 1810 and 1820 the population of Waltham increased 60 percent as a result of the establishment and expansion of the Boston Manufacturing Company. Within a few decades of the company's founding it became the heart of Waltham, providing a comfortable work environment, housing, a school, a fire engine, and a social and religious center for its employees.

In 1819, the Boston Manufacturing Company purchased land belonging to the Waltham Cotton and Wool Company as well as the land between the factories. The company established its bleachery on this property down river from the main factory. It also built River Street, which ran along the Charles River, to connect the buildings.

In 1843, the Fitchburg Railroad laid its tracks to run by the Boston Manufacturing Company. This was the first railroad linking Waltham to Boston. Its use as a means of delivering and receiving goods for manufacturing purposes promoted an industrial boom that changed the community from one of small farms to a manufacturing base. The Carter Street Depot, shown here, stood between the Waltham Common and the mills.

In 1789, John Boies erected the first dam across the Charles River in Waltham to power his paper mill. In 1812, the Boston Manufacturing Company elevated the dam to accommodate its business. In the right corner of this photograph are the mills of the Boston Manufacturing Company.

The river supplied power for the mills as the torrent over the dam shows here. The founders of the Boston Manufacturing Company realized that they needed more power to expand their operations and the Merrimac River, approximately 30 miles to the north, offered the needed energy. In the 1820s, they founded the Merrimac Manufacturing Company and the Town of Lowell.

The Moody Street Bridge has undergone many changes over time. In 1921, the City of Waltham hired George M. Bryne to construct a wider, stronger bridge of concrete. Workers in this photograph are putting together the new bridge while a horse and buggy travels over the old.

In the early 19th century, the Boston Manufacturing Company also owned land on the south side of the Charles River. This land could only be reached by boat from the company mills on the north side. In 1847, the first bridge across the river at this location allowed Waltham residents to establish living quarters on the South Side, which was then part of the town of Newton. In the 1920s residents walked across the Moody Street Bridge or used motorcars to travel across the river. Trolley tracks ran through the center of the street.

In 1820, Dr. Samuel Dana organized the Newton Chemical Works with support from Patrick Tracy Jackson of the Boston Manufacturing Company. The company manufactured sulfuric and bleaching acids. In 1849, Waltham annexed from Newton the land on which the factory stood. Both towns recognized the company's ties to Waltham's growing industry and supported the purchase and sale of what became Waltham's South Side. The area surrounding the company became known as the "Chemistry."

The Boston Manufacturing Company offered low pay to unskilled workers and there was a high turnover of employees. The company relied heavily on young women between the ages of 18 and 25 who came to make money for the short term and then left. The mill was finally shut down in 1930 after 116 years of continuous operation.

Two
Religion

The area near Lexington and Lincoln Streets encompasses the district known as Piety Corner in Waltham. Inhabited mainly by the Sandersons and Livermores in the 18th century, this settlement received its name from these "pious" folks. The families were very influential in town as well as in church affairs. In fact, almost all of the early leading members of the first church resided in the Piety Corner area.

In 1720, Waltham residents set up the first house of worship in Waltham territory near the present Lyman Estate. The First Church ordained Samuel Ripley in 1809. He was the third reverend to preach in town and stayed until he was called to Concord in 1846. Some congregation members split with Ripley's church in 1820 to form the Second Religious Society.

Beginning under the direction of Reverend Sewall Harding in 1825, the Trinitarian Society was the third church established in Waltham. Their first house of worship stood at the corner of Main and Heard Streets. In 1870, the parish renamed itself the First Congregational Church and erected a new building on Main Street. In 1914, the City of Waltham built the public library across the street from it.

The First Church of Waltham reunited with the second church in 1838. The newly formed organization called itself the Independent Congregational Society and constructed a new building for worship on the corner of School and Church Streets. In 1866, the congregation renamed itself the First Parish Church. A fire destroyed this original church in 1932 with losses estimated between $75,000 and $100,000. Passersby in this photograph visit the site of the destruction.

Thomas Hill served as the first minister at the Independent Congregational Society from 1845 to 1860. Reverend Hill was very active in the field of education and worked with Thomas Mann to reform the American educational system. He served as chairman of the Waltham School Board and eventually left the city to become president of Antioch College and later of Harvard University.

In 1830, Waltham Catholics held their first mass in a shed on Church Street. The original St. Mary's Church also stood on Church Street and burned to the ground in 1848. Reverend Patrick Flood oversaw the building of the second St. Mary's Church on School Street, shown in this photograph without its steeple next to the church rectory. St. Mary's was the only Catholic church in Waltham until 1894.

The Ancient Order of Hibernians was an Irish-Catholic group first organized in Waltham in 1875. It established itself in the United States 39 years earlier with the purpose of promoting Christian charity and the independence of Ireland. The organization held events for the members, provided them with benefits, and raised money for charity. In 1952, some AOH members posed for this photograph taken by E.M. Logan for the local newspaper.

In 1894, the French-speaking population in Waltham established its own church. Members held services in a temporary chapel called Lafayette Hall on the third floor of the Geoffrion residence. The home at 11 Noonan Street served St. Joseph's congregation until congregants purchased Christ Church Episcopal—located on Central Street—in 1895.

Organized in 1849, Christ Church Episcopal sold its church building to St. Joseph's 46 years later. Various halls then housed Christ Church services until the new building on Main Street was completed in 1897. A.M. Ryan, noted Waltham historian, drew this picture, which he believed to depict the original Christ Church building.

The Ascension Episcopal Church was located on Moody Street and dedicated in 1882. It began its services as a mission under the charge of Rev. Thomas F. Fales of Christ Church. In 1888, the church voted to become an independent parish. Those who worshipped there were generally from working-class families on the South Side of the city.

Donated by the Boston Manufacturing Company to its Italian employees, the original Church of the Sacred Heart of Jesus stood on River Street. The church shown here once served the Lutherans, but beginning in 1922 it accommodated the Italian Catholic population of Waltham. It offered services in Italian and now serves as a community center for its members. In 1959, a new church was built beside the old to accommodate the growing parish.

Members of the Swedenborgian parish, also known as the Church of the New Jerusalem, held their first services at the Calvin Clark House. The followers of Swedish scientist Emanuel Swedenborg erected their church building in 1860 on Lexington Street at Piety Corner. After about 90 years, the Swedish Covenant Congregational Church bought the center and worships there today.

In 1837, the Second Religious Society sold its church to the Methodists. The building in this photograph stood at the corner of Moody and Main Streets, where parishioners moved it after the town purchased the original site across the street for a Common. After a fire in 1860, the congregation erected a second place of worship at the same location. Fleet Bank now stands here.

In 1919, after worshipping in private homes and rented halls for many years, the Jewish community of Waltham bought the land at the corner of Harvard and Russell Streets for their temple. They named their building the Beth Israel Jewish Community Center in 1925 and replaced it in 1950 with a larger synagogue designed to accommodate their growing numbers. Here the Hebrew schoolchildren stand by the back door of the new center for a group portrait.

Incorporated in 1890, the First Evangelical Lutheran Church received property on River Street from the Boston Manufacturing Company. Members worshipped in a church they erected here until 1920, when they moved to Eddy Street and constructed a new building.

The Waltham Evangelical Free Church incorporated in 1952 and dedicated its house of worship on Bruce Road in 1955. At its inception, this church was composed primarily of people of Norwegian descent. It overflowed with children attending Sunday school early in its history.

The Catholic population of the city grew and in 1909 formed a second parish named St. Charles Borromeo. Parishioners held Sunday services outdoors on Hall Street before the church was built. In 1916, the new building opened on the corner of Hall and Cushing Streets. Eventually, two more Catholic parishes were established: Our Lady's on Trapelo Road in 1930 and St. Jude's on lower Main Street in 1949.

The First Presbyterian Church organized in 1893 at a meeting in the Beth Eden Baptist Church. The parish members held services in various halls before building their own church in 1898 at the corner of Beech and Alder Streets. A photographer captured this image before the church steeple toppled in the hurricane of 1938. The parish renovated the church in the 1960s.

In 1852, 24 people organized the First Baptist Church. They worshipped in Rumford Hall until 1856, when they dedicated their house of worship. Francis Buttrick constructed the new building at the corner of Felton and Moody Streets, which was eventually replaced with a new church on Lexington Street. In 1887, some members of this church broke off to form Beth Eden Baptist Church on the South Side.

Organized in 1887, Beth Eden Baptist Church was one of the first houses of worship located on the south side of the Charles River in Waltham. The congregation erected a church on Maple Street in 1891. A fire in 1908 necessitated the rebuilding of the church and at this time, the architect incorporated a space for the organ shown here. Music is an important part of the church services and is provided by choir members and a soloist.

In 1888, the Immanuel Methodist Episcopal Church formed with members who left the First Methodist Church. The congregation erected the church shown here on the corner of Moody and Cherry Streets, where a cornfield previously stood. The two Methodist churches reunited in 1938. In this photograph, worshippers and residents easily navigate the snow-covered streets by sleigh.

Three

Education

Built in 1775, the original Pond End School was one of the first school buildings located in Waltham. Erected in 1850 on Winter Street, the building shown here was the second Pond End School. It comprised one room, but later expanded to two. In 1914, the Piety Corner Club bought the school to serve as a clubhouse. The club moved the building to its present site at the corner of Bacon Street and Worcester Lane.

In 1912, the city erected a new Pond End School building adjacent to the old. This unusual photograph shows the two buildings side-by-side before the Piety Corner Club moved the old school.

Established in 1883 as the Bacon Street School, the Plympton School began as a four-room building. It stood on land that once was a part of respected town landowner Thomas Ruggles Plympton's 75-acre farm. The Waltham Emery Wheel Company was located near the school along the railroad tracks.

Around 1817, the Boston Manufacturing Company erected the Elm Street School for the children of its employees. The school stood on the northeast end of Elm Street near what is now Waltham Common. When the manufacturing company erected a new school, shown below, this one became a residence. It was demolished in 1949.

In 1829, the Boston Manufacturing Company erected the Stone School to replace the original schoolhouse. The school was larger than its predecessor to accommodate the mill's growing numbers. Located on River Street just south of the railroad, the building was maintained by the company for education until the town built district schools about 1860. The company converted it to a paint shop at that time.

The Thomas Hill School stood on the site of the old Congregational church at the corner of Main and Heard Streets. Waltham architect H.W. Hartwell designed this building, in addition to many others in this book. When erected in 1881, the brick schoolhouse accommodated 224 pupils. It expanded in 1913 and closed in 1977.

The Whittemore School faculty and staff of the 1952–53 school year posed outside the schoolhouse for this photograph. The city erected the building in 1927. In the 1950s, drastic growth in student population necessitated the construction of more educational facilities and a building project was begun.

In 1869, this building was the first structure established exclusively as a high school in the town of Waltham. Previously, the town offered upper-level classes in a building that also served as town administrative offices and a grammar school. Located on the northeast corner of Church and School Streets, the new high school served the students until the city erected a new building in 1903. The town demolished the old building in 1935.

Waltham built its second high school on property taken by eminent domain. The school stood on School Street opposite Liberty Street, adjoining the property of the first high school. Here workers are shown breaking ground for the school.

Samuel Patch designed the second Waltham High School. In 1935, the building expanded with east and west wings. A new gymnasium, a cafeteria, and another classroom wing were added in the early 1960s. When the city constructed the new high school on Lexington Street in 1969, the old high school became the Central Middle School. The building is no longer used by students and is being redesigned as a community center.

The Usen Castle now serves as a student dormitory for Brandeis University on South Street. Built by Middlesex College founder Dr. John Hall Smith in 1928, the building was inspired by Ireland's Cavendish Castle. Fashioned in the Gothic style and constructed of fieldstone and concrete, the castle encompasses 50,000 square feet of space.

The 1931 graduating class from Middlesex Medical School gathered in front of "the Castle" for their class portrait. Established by John Hall Smith in 1927, Middlesex College of Medicine and Surgery stood on one of the first tracts of land settled in Waltham. Once owned by Dr. Baker, the property was used as a tuberculosis hospital before the college purchased it.

SCIENCE HALL, BRANDEIS UNIVERSITY, WALTHAM, MASSACHUSETTS   4418

Brandeis University opened in 1948 as a Jewish-sponsored secular school of higher learning. The campus is located on 250 acres of land that once belonged to Middlesex University. Shown here is Science Hall, which was once the School of Veterinary Medicine under Middlesex University.

In 1888, St. Mary's Parish dedicated St. Joseph's Parochial School, shown here. The building sat in a cluster of church-owned buildings including the rectory, convent, brothers' house, and the church itself. In 1923, the church enlarged its educational facilities and erected a new high school building on Lexington Street, which closed in 1973.

In 1860, the Church of the New Jerusalem opened a school for boys and girls that supported its religious philosophies. A few years later, the parish moved the New Church School from the west end of their chapel to the new adjacent building shown here. Located in Piety Corner on land originally belonging to the Clark farm, the schoolhouse resembles a Greek cross. The educational institution continues today as the Chapel Hill-Chauncy Hall School.

The many hills in Waltham are a great boon for winter recreation. The children in this photograph are shown sledding near the Chapel Hill School in 1951.

In 1912, the New Church School became the Chapel Hill School for Girls. The Boston-based Chauncy Hall School for Boys moved to Waltham in 1971 and joined with the girls' school. The co-educational collaboration was named the Chapel Hill-Chauncy Hall School.

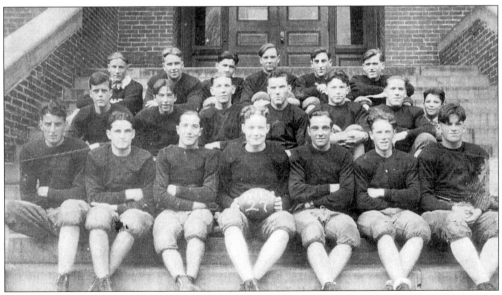

Waltham High School supported a football team beginning in 1895. The team had many winning seasons over the years, including 1926 and 1928. The 1927 high school football team, shown here, was plagued with injuries and had a rather unsuccessful season.

In 1955, at the height of America's quiz-show craze, elementary school students from the Thomas Hill School in Waltham competed in the Boston Globe/WCOP "Quizdown."

Drama clubs and the theater have always played an important role in Waltham. The city is home to two renowned drama groups, the Reagle Players and the Hovey Players. The high school is also very involved in productions. Here the 1925 high school drama cast of *Peter Pan* is posing in costume.

Built in 1920, North Junior High School housed seventh, eighth, and ninth graders who were taken from the Waltham grammar schools and the high school. The concept of a junior high school education was new in the United States. Waltham educators explored new theories to redesign their curriculum. This School Street building was the first in Waltham to accommodate students on this level.

South Junior High School opened on Moody Street in November 1923 while the building was still under construction. One hundred forty-three students filled classrooms while workers finished the auditorium and other rooms. A formal opening of the school took place in January 1924. This building helped Waltham's South Side adopt the new junior high curriculum.

Four
The Watch City

In 1904, the Waltham Watch Company baseball team—the Jewels—was crowned champion of the Waltham Factory League. The winners defeated the Hair Spring, Flat Steel, and American teams. The Jewels won a silver championship cup offered by the Waltham newspaper, *The Free Press Tribune*. The players with the most base hits, homeruns, and runs won boxes of cigars.

The Waltham Watch Company was the first in the world to mass-produce watches. It was also the first company in America to successfully compete against English and Swiss manufacturers. In 1853, the business began sales as the Boston Watch Company in Roxbury under Aaron L. Dennison, Edward Howard, and Samuel Curtis. The company moved to Waltham in 1854 and its original Waltham factory, shown here, stood along the Charles River.

The watch company offered higher wages, had more semi-skilled and skilled workers, and had a lower employee turnover than the Boston Manufacturing Company. Many prominent men in the city served the factory, including members of the government and clergy. Unlike the Boston Manufacturing Company that relied on women, the watch company depended equally on male and female employees. Here, men and women sit back to back in the plate department of the factory putting together movements.

The Waltham Watch Company started building houses on company land as soon as it moved to Waltham. The owners systematically laid out streets around the homes. They also built and maintained two large boarding houses. The Adams House, shown here and located at 94 Adams Street, was a women-only boarding establishment. The Shawmut House rented to bachelors.

The Boston Watch Company established itself on the former Bemis farm property. In 1857, Royal E. Robbins bought the company. He changed the company name to the American Watch Company, which was eventually changed to the Waltham Watch Company. In the 19th century, famous Waltham photographer H.F. Warren captured the rural landscape of the town behind the watch company in this photograph. The building's reflection is visible in the Charles River.

The dust in Roxbury was hazardous to the fine mechanisms of time-keeping devices. In Waltham, the company set up Robbins Park to protect its products from being contaminated by small particles and to offer the factory setting more light and air. Named after company owner Royal E. Robbins, the park also offered Waltham residents the benefit of a beautiful public area. Visible behind the park in this photograph is the clock tower of the Waltham Watch Company.

WALTHAM
8-Day Timepieces

The Waltham Watch Company created Waltham Eight Day Timepieces for travelers. These chronometers withstood jarring and adverse weather conditions, making them ideal for use in automobiles, motorboats, and limousines. This particular model is housed in a polished mahogany weatherproof box with brass trimmings. The watch company also produced wristwatches and railroad watches.

A footbridge was built across the Charles River just north of the watch company land in 1882. A year earlier the town voted down a proposal to extend Prospect Street over the river. The footbridge was not very sturdy and remained in use only until 1889.

When the noon bell struck for dinner, men and women emerged from the watch factory for the mid-day meal. The Newton trolley ran down the center of the street where workers cross Crescent Street to Robbins Park.

The Waltham Watch Company trained engineers and watchmakers in their own school. They did not necessarily require previous experience. The men shown here are taking part in a nine-month training course. During their instructional period, trainees received pay at the lowest company wage and prepared for advanced technical work. Generally, the few men who were hired outright for their skills came from watch factories in Europe.

People recognized the Waltham Watch Company as the best in the world for making accurate and dependable products. The company's advertisement campaigns showed people from all over the world relying on Waltham watches. This particular ad shows Italians being encouraged to choose the American watch over its European counterparts.

The Waltham Watch Company sits along the Charles River. Many men lived on the other side of the waterway and boated to work in warm weather. When the river froze they would walk to work on the ice.

The Waltham Watch Company soon had many competitors in the United States. Edward Howard was one of the original founders of the Boston Watch Company. When Royal E. Robbins bought the company and moved it to Waltham, Howard returned to Roxbury to start the Howard Watch and Clock Company. In 1903, the Howard Company also moved to Waltham. Howard Watch employees are shown in this photograph in 1916 on their annual outing.

Companies formed to provide the watch factories with tools for making their products. The American Watch Tool Company began producing watchmakers' lathes in 1872. A small group of employees from the Waltham Watch Company began this business in Boston, a year later moving to Waltham.

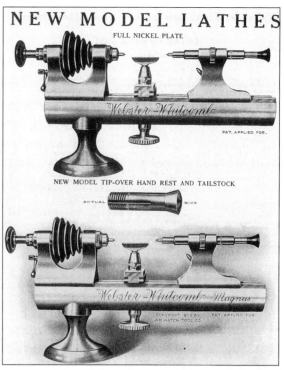

The United States Watch Company was another Waltham Watch Company competitor. It began as the Waltham Watch Tool Company in 1879 and went public in 1882 under the United States Watch Company name. The factory erected on Charles Street became the property of the Howard Watch Company.

In 1911, one has a great view looking east down the Charles River from the top of the Waltham Watch Company. Prospect Street runs across the river and churches are visible in the background along the Main Street area of the city.

Five

Main Street

This group gathered on Main Street in front of Rumford Hall in the 1890s. Located at the corner of Main and Elm Streets, the building occupied the present site of Waltham City Hall. Structures along Main Street were often decorated for events with flags and banners as this one is adorned. The people here seem to wait for the arrival of a parade.

The Boston Manufacturing Company formed the Rumford Institute to promote adult learning. It was the earliest institution of its kind in the state and perhaps the first in the country. Erected in 1827, Rumford Hall hosted many famous lecturers, including Nathaniel P. Banks and Ralph Waldo Emerson. In 1850, The town began holding government meetings there. Soon after, they purchased the building from the Boston Manufacturing Company for use as a town hall.

Organized in 1836, the Waltham National Bank stood at 637 Main Street on the corner of Lexington Street. Incorporated as a state bank in 1864, its building also housed the public library and town administrative offices for a short while. In 1888, the bank erected a new building on the site to serve as the headquarters for both the Waltham Savings and Waltham National Banks.

In 1798, John Clark occupied the farmhouse that once stood at this site. David Smith bought the property and erected a tavern here in the 19th century. The building changed hands and names many times. Its final incarnation was as the Central House, shown here, before the City of Waltham bought the property in 1914. The city's public library now stands on this site.

Main Street was the principle thoroughfare west of Boston in the 18th and early 19th centuries. Many inns and taverns were established along this route to accommodate travelers. Built by John Ball in 1753 at 244 Weston Street, which branches off Main Street, the Stratton Tavern burned in 1893. It was the last of Waltham's famous inns to stand.

Nathaniel Plympton Rutter and William Rideout established the Rutter and Rideout hardware store in 1893. They worked at the corner of Main and Hammond Streets until their partnership dissolved in 1899. Rutter then carried on the business alone.

This 1917 photograph shows Ching Sing Laundry, located between Church and Liberty Streets among the many other service shops that once stood on Main Street. There were 16 laundries in Waltham at this time, including five on Main Street.

Established in 1865, the Waltham Public Library included the library collections of the Rumford Institute, the Waltham Agricultural Society, and the Waltham Social Library. The town library originally shared a building with the Waltham National Bank. In 1878, it moved to the Welch building shown here. A boys' table separated the children from the adults so that the adults wouldn't be disturbed.

The city built its public library in 1914 with funds bequeathed by Francis Buttrick. In 1917, the town decorated the building, originally known as the Buttrick Library, for Flag Day celebrations. This edifice was remodeled and expanded in 1994.

Focusing on Central Block, one sees Johnson Drugs and the Hansen Smoke Shop. Originally called Miller Block, the building was erected in 1856. The upper floors served as a hotel and Henry Sawyer's variety store was on the ground floor. Other businesses and offices occupied the building, including John Stark's original tool shop.

Taken in 1905, this photograph looks toward the west down Main Street. Across from Waltham Common is Central Block with Johnson Drugs and its striped awning. On the left of the photograph is the corner of Main and Moody Streets. The Methodist building, which replaced the Methodist church, is visible here. Further up the street, one can see the spire of the First Congregational Church.

Workers in this photograph remodel the barn once owned by tavern keeper David Smith based on the designs of noted Waltham architect Ida Annah Ryan. Workers also moved the structure from Main Street to Hammond Street. The building now serves as apartments and stands near the renovated Prospect House. Miss Ryan was the first woman to earn a Master's degree from MIT.

Main Street thrived as a retail and entertainment center in the early 20th century. People parked their cars along the street to go to the five-and-dime stores and various restaurants. The A&P Supermarket, located on the left in this photograph, stood near the site of the current Shaw's Supermarket. A bowling alley also stood along the road.

The scaffolding around the new city hall during its construction in 1926 accentuates the building's many windows. The limestone façade is adorned with symbolic statuary and the copper roof is visible here.

Dedicated on January 6, 1927, the current city hall replaced Rumford Hall as the center of government. The architects of the building were Kilham, Hopkins, and Greeling. The public previewed the building before the opening ceremony, which took place in the evening. Members of the government, former officials, veterans, and other honored guests attended the festivities that were held in the city council chamber.

PROGRAM OF EXERCISES
Attending the Dedication of
NEW CITY HALL BUILDING
WALTHAM, MASSACHUSETTS

Thursday Evening, January 6, 1927, at eight o'clock

INVOCATION . . . Rev. Francis E. Webster
Turning over of the Building by the Architect
Acceptance by His Honor the Mayor

Presentation of National and State Flags by Woman's Relief Corps
Commander Samuel E. Clark, Post 29, G. A. R. and Mrs. Amanda Wheeler, President W. R. C., F. P. H. Rogers 25

Acceptance by President Alexander R. Smith, Jr., of the City Council.

Presentation of City Flag by Waltham Post 156, American Legion, Captain John E. Branth, U. S. W. V. and American Legion.
Acceptance by Councillor Edmund A. Broe

ORATION . . . Honorable John M. Gibbs
Justice of the Second District Court of Eastern Middlesex

BENEDICTION . . . . Rev. Peter J. Walsh

IN THE LIBRARY—Reception to the Mayor of Waltham
Honorable Henry Foster Beal and Mrs. Beal

Inspection of Building under guidance of the Boy Scouts, assisted by the Departments

Orchestral Concert, 7.30 to 8.00, and during the evening.
Flowers and Decorations donated by Harvey F. Whitemore.
Inspection of Building, 3 to 5

56

Banks Square on Main Street received its name in honor of Waltham hero Nathaniel P. Banks. Looking west from the Square toward Weston, we see the cobblestone streets down which trolley cars ran. This photograph appeared in the 1928 City of Waltham Annual Reports. It demonstrated the need for street resurfacing with asphalt.

Yetten Motor Corporation, located at 613 Main Street, was one of many automotive dealers in the city. In 1923 there were over 20 dealerships with at least 4 on Main Street alone.

Located near the current post office on Main Street, Waltham Baby Hospital opened in 1900 and incorporated in 1902. At the start, Waltham's beloved Dr. Alfred Worcester was one of hospital's most active physicians. The Waltham Visiting Nurses assumed management of the organization in 1947. In 1972, the institution dissolved and became part of Waltham Hospital.

The Hospital Buildings, Waltham, Mass.

In 1885, Drs. Alfred Worcester and Edward Cutler started a private hospital and a small nurses' training school. Known as the Waltham Cottage Hospital and located on Main Street, the organization merged with the public hospital in 1888. In 1892, the hospital dedicated their new complex shown here and built near South Street.

Six

Moody Street and Waltham Common

In the 17th century, the Waltham Common property was privately owned and divided among three men. The Boston Manufacturing Company bought the land in the early 19th century and built mills on the southernmost part near the Charles River. The company gave the northern grounds to the Second Religious Society to erect their church, shown here.

This photograph from 1888 shows the Waltham Common soon after the city developed it for recreational use. On the left side is a bandstand erected in 1863. In the background and across Moody Street is the Methodist church. Also visible are some of the many trees on Waltham Common. In the 1850s, they numbered 362 and included elms, maples, chestnuts, sycamores, ashes, oaks, pines, cedars, and other less popular varieties. The hurricane of 1938 toppled many of them.

Built in 1884, the Harrington Block on the right was named after bleachery employee Charles Harrington. Though considered at first to be too far from the center of the city, this masonry building at 376–390 Moody Street became an important part of the Moody Street commercial district.

Located on Moody Street, the variety store of Cone and McClure sold toys, candy, and household goods. In the 1880s, Arthur McClure stands near his delivery horse.

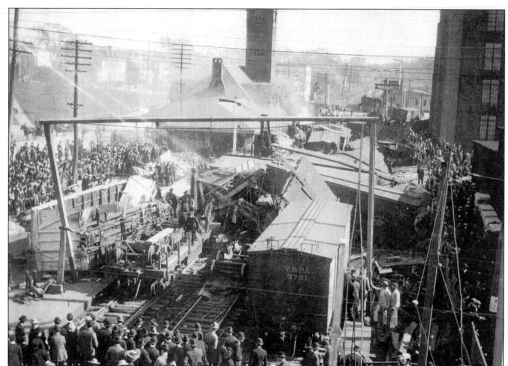

On October 22, 1900, two trains collided just east of Moody Street. Fitchburg Railroad employee Leonard Cooper was killed. An article about the crash in the local paper indicated that the cause of the accident was a faulty signal. This scene attracted the attention of many photographers who clamored on the rooftops of nearby buildings to get their shots. The event heightened a city council debate on the abolition of grade crossings.

Hall and Lyon Company was a prominent pharmacy in the 19th century. Number 117 Moody Street, which was renumbered 265–271 in 1923, was named Hall's Corner after Henry C. Hall, who ran his business there with George C. Lyon beginning in 1868. The owners set up a soda fountain in addition to their apothecary business.

The Central Dry Goods Store stood at 107–115 Moody Street. The business sold clothing, utensils, crockery, teas, and other household items. Occupying 12,500 square feet, the property later became part of the block owned by Grover Cronin Inc. It is now the home of the Cronin's Landing apartment complex.

Originally called "The Lane to the River," Moody Street ran from Main Street to the Charles River. The road soon stretched across the waterway to accommodate residents on the South Side of town. The bridge shown here is the predecessor to the 1921 bridge shown on p. 13. In this photograph, we see all the forms of traffic that the Moody Street Bridge has handled over the years, including people walking, horse-drawn carriages, trains, and cars.

Main Street housed most of Waltham's retail establishments until Moody Street began to boom in the 1890s. Even after that time, most of south Moody Street remained residential into the 20th century. Residential buildings stand across the street from small retail establishments on the unpaved Moody Street, shown here. Sidewalks allowed shoppers and residents to stroll in comfort.

The retail boom on Moody Street brought chain stores such as Woolworth's at 299–301 Moody Street in the early 20th century. To the right of Woolworth's is the Lincoln building with its window awnings. Built in the 1870s, this structure is one of the oldest on Moody Street. Its most famous tenant was the Parke Snow department store, which occupied the site from 1919 to 1973.

In 1880, attorney Charles Welch built the Welch Block on the corner of Moody and Charles Streets. This building stood three stories high and housed the Masonic Hall. The structure also housed the Waltham Public Library for about 30 years. The architect designed the first floor specifically to accommodate 20,000 books.

In 1889, Hamblin L. Hovey erected the Parmenter Block at the corner of Moody and Felton Streets. The Parmenter building design accommodated three stores on the ground floor with offices and an auditorium and banquet hall on the two other levels. Jonas Willis Parmenter was Hovey's father-in-law and the inspiration for the block's name.

An aerial view of the east end of the Common taken by Watch Credit Line Fairchild Aerial Surveys, Inc. shows the corner of Main and Elm Streets. City hall stands on the site of the old Rumford Hall. Looking north of Main Street in the 1920s, we see the clock and spire of the First Parish Church. The massive building across Church Street to the right is the old Waltham High School (Central Middle School). The "I"-shaped Government Center stands to the left across Common Street. The Waldorf Theater is located at the center of Elm Street on the bottom right of the photograph.

The city erected the Moody Street Fire Station in 1891 and renovated it in 1901 after a fire. Horses pulled the original fire equipment housed here, but in 1912, the department purchased its first motorized vehicles for Moody Street while other stations still operated with horses. In 1987, a modernization project conducted on the building allowed the station to continue operating up to the present day.

When Moody Street began to develop as a thriving business and retail district its architecture changed. Developers replaced old wooden frame structures with modern brick buildings. In this photograph, construction begins on a new building.

Parades down Moody Street were a popular attraction for Waltham residents. During its heyday, Moody Street was also alive with department and chain stores. Thom McAn and Woolworth's were among those in the area. Woolworth's opened in 1905 as a five-and-dime store. It was the first store of its kind in Waltham and was open for 92 years.

Grover Cronin sponsored the most parades in Waltham. In this photograph, parade participants march past three of Waltham's major department stores: JC Penney, Sears, and Cronin's. Representing a major shopping center before malls took off, Waltham's 20th-century stores clustered on Moody Street. In 1989, Cronin's was the last of the department stores to close. It encompassed a whole city block and provided ample parking, making it a hotspot for shoppers.

Seven
Waltham People

On Armistice Day in 1935, Waltham thanked its World War I soldiers with a parade that ran 2 miles through the city. The governor of Massachusetts, Waltham's mayor, and American Legion officials observed from the reviewing stand. Those celebrating honored American Legion Commander John H. Walsh, shown here at Hall's Corner handing flowers to drum major Dorothy Slamin Hill.

Founded in 1937, the Waltham Boys Club first met in the Asbury Temple at the corner of Main and Moody Streets where the Methodist church once stood. The temple was the home of many organizations and the boys club members decided that they needed their own space. They opened their own building on Exchange Street near the main branch of the public library in 1952. To raise money for the new building, heavyweight boxing champion Jack Dempsey made appearances in Waltham. In this photograph, Dempsey signs autographs for area youth.

In 1871, Waltham put its first steam fire engine into service. Built by Manchester Locomotive Works of New Hampshire, the engine worked with hand- or horse-drawn travel. Retired members of the Neptune Hand Tub Company worked the equipment, which they housed at the Spruce Street fire station. In 1872, they shipped the engine to Boston for service during the Great Boston Fire.

Hose Company Number 3 on Moody Street received the second motorized vehicle used in Waltham. The engine went into service in 1912. When an alarm sounded, a driver picked up the volunteer firemen who worked at the watch factory. Shown here in 1918, Hose Company Number 3 stands for a portrait with their engine. Waltham's first firemen volunteered in 1817 for Waltham Engine Company Number 1 and worked with a fire engine purchased by the Boston Manufacturing Company.

Social clubs and fraternal organizations were popular in Waltham during the 19th and early 20th centuries. The United Order of Turks was one such group.

The Waltham police have served the city since 1852, when one officer guarded the lockup located on the corner of Main and Elm Streets. The force was officially approved as a city department in 1885. In this photograph, Raymond Thompson wears the uniform worn by officers during 1917, when police were first using motorized vehicles.

In 1958, John F. Kennedy visited the *Waltham News Tribune* newsroom with Editor Thomas J. Murphy, who stands to his left. The newspaper is the successor to a legacy of other Waltham presses. Established in 1882, it followed on the heels of such Waltham publications as the *Waltham Sentinel*, the *Waltham Free Press*, and the *Waltham Daily Times*. Local Waltham papers dating from 1830 are preserved on microfilm at the Waltham Public Library.

Persuaded by Patrick Tracy Jackson and Paul Moody, Nathan Appleton invested in the upstart Boston Manufacturing Company in 1813 and served on the company's board of directors. Living and working in Boston as a merchant, he represented that city in the House of Representatives five times. He also served in Congress beginning in 1831. In this capacity, he aimed to support the business enterprises of American manufacturers.

The 19th amendment passed the U.S. House and Senate in June of 1919. It then went to the states for ratification. Massachusetts was the eighth state to accept it. Women traveled down the streets of Waltham rallying for the cause, riding in a truck with signs painted by Waltham historian and city employee Albert Morse Ryan.

Christopher Gore is noted for his service to Massachusetts. He fought in the American Revolution, served as a commissioner in the ratification of the Federal Constitution, and worked as governor of the commonwealth from 1809 to 1810. In 1786, Gore built a mansion in Waltham for his family. Soon after, he established business interests here, building a dam and paper mill on the Charles River.

Many important political figures passed through Waltham on their way to Boston in the 18th century. General Burgoyne's army traveled along the Boston Post Road (Main Street) to Cambridge during the Revolutionary War. This commemorative plaque once graced the corner of Main and Grant Streets in front of the Prospect House. When it was taken down in 1912, the Dorothy Brewer Chapter of the Daughters of the American Revolution received a section of the 220-year-old tree.

The town of Waltham sent seven hundred men to military service during the Civil War. Captain Samuel Lyman Ryan served in the 30th regiment of Massachusetts volunteers. He received an award for his bravery in service. When wounded at the siege of Blakeley, Alabama, Ryan left the hospital early in order to lead his troops into another battle. Letters he wrote home to his mother are housed in the Waltham Public Library.

Born on River Street in 1816, Nathaniel Prentiss Banks worked in the cotton mill as a bobbin boy and was largely self-educated. He served in the U.S. Congress for many years, was Speaker of the House in 1856, and was elected governor of Massachusetts in 1857. He helped establish the United States Republican Party. At the outbreak of the American Civil War, President Lincoln appointed Banks as a major general. He commanded defenses in Virginia; Washington, D.C.; and New Orleans.

Nathan Warren was a prosperous Waltham businessman and politician. Upon graduation from Waltham High School, he opened a dry goods business in Boston. After serving in the 45th Massachusetts Volunteers during the Civil War, Warren entered the shipping trade in Waltham and the insurance business soon thereafter. He was state legislator for Waltham from 1880 to 1887. He also served on the boards of the city library and historical society and was vice president of the savings bank.

Well-known in Waltham business circles, Francis Buttrick was the largest single non-corporate property owner in Waltham in the late 19th century and was the principle benefactor for the construction of the public library. His wealth was the result of investments in the growing industrial and urbanizing town.

In 1873, Waltham started building its first pumping station. Located in the newer section of Mount Feake Cemetery, Pumping Station Number One accommodated the growing South Side. Taking water from Quinobequin Cove on the Charles River, the pumping station supplied water that wells could no longer adequately provide to the residents. Workers here erect the brickwork necessary for the station. Many Italian immigrants in Massachusetts gained employment doing this type of work.

On September 27, 1950, 46 draftees from Newton and Waltham gathered on the steps of Waltham City Hall for a portrait. Two hundred fifty people crowded the city council chambers for a special ceremony to wish the men farewell. In this photograph, some of the men hold duffel bags of toiletries and other items donated by volunteer contributors.

The American Legion Band in Waltham began in 1948 under the direction of Dorothy Slamin Hill, who was a national champion drum major and a Waltham native. Starting with only 12 members, the band became an instant sensation and their numbers quickly grew. The group has become legendary for its trips around the world, including a 1990 trip to the Soviet Union. The band played in Red Square as the first non-communist participants of that country's annual May Day parade.

A member of Beth Eden Baptist Church and a founding member of the Waltham Council of Churches, Lillian Shirley tolled the bells of her chapel to remember the U.S. hostages held in Iran from 1979 to 1980. Shirley worked as an English teacher at Waltham High School and later served on the school committee.

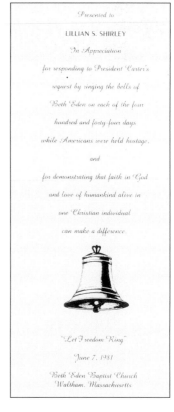

Presented to

LILLIAN S. SHIRLEY

In Appreciation

for responding to President Carter's

request by ringing the bells of

Beth Eden on each of the four

hundred and forty-four days

while Americans were held hostage,

and

for demonstrating that faith in God

and love of humankind alive in

one Christian individual

can make a difference.

"Let Freedom Ring"

June 7, 1981

Beth Eden Baptist Church
Waltham, Massachusetts

President Reagan honored Lillian Sundin Shirley in 1981 for her work in recognizing the hostages. She climbed the steps of the Beth Eden bell tower every day for each of the 444 days the hostages were held in the Middle East.

Waltham veterans from the Civil War, the Spanish-American War, the Mexican Border Campaign, and World War I gathered for this portrait on the Waltham Common in 1929.

Arthur Hansen served with the National Guard during World War I and received honors for distinguished service. Hansen went on to serve in the Massachusetts House of Representatives for nine years. Waltham residents elected him as mayor in 1938 and he died in office in 1942.

Waltham residents planted Victory Gardens to support their country. This photograph shows Mary W. Barnes working in her vegetable garden in 1919.

James Fahey wrote the best-selling *Pacific War Diary*. Thomas Murphy served as editor of the *Waltham News Tribune*. They stand together in this photograph at a ceremony honoring Fahey. In 1963, his book based on his experiences during World War II aboard the USS *Montpelier* was published. Fahey worked as a sanitation worker in Waltham and donated his book profits to charity.

In 1885, Waltham's first nurses learned by practicing with a doctor in a patient's home. Three years later, the Waltham Training School for Nurses opened in association with the Waltham Cottage Hospital. In the 1930s, nurses began to receive training at the Waltham Hospital. This photograph, taken in the 1950s, shows some of the nurses at the hospital.

Jonas Willis Parmenter first worked in the bleachery and later entered the coal business. He made a fortune in coal and lumber and passed the business on to his son-in-law Hamblin L. Hovey. Hovey's home at 542 Main Street later became the Parmenter Rest Home.

Established in 1842, the Waltham Ice Company was a branch of one of the first ice companies in Massachusetts. By 1891 the Peterson family ran the business, which produced 10,000 tons of ice for its customers. Fifteen horses pulled the wagons until the company purchased trucks in the 20th century. Two men stand near a Peterson ice truck in this photograph.

Eight

Recreation

Located on Prospect Street and built in 1899, Nuttings-on-the-Charles hosted dances, political meetings, wedding receptions, civic banquets, trade shows, boxing and wrestling matches, roller skating, and school proms. It opened as a dance hall in 1914 and provided a stage for musicians such as Guy Lombardo, Louis Armstrong, Rudy Vallee, and Benny Goodman. In 1916, the Knights of Columbus honored former President William Howard Taft here, and many other famous people appeared at Nuttings during its history. The building was used as a storage facility for Parke Snow department store beginning in 1959, but burned to the water line in June 1961.

The Waltham Music Hall Company purchased this site on Elm Street in December 1879, providing Waltham with its first "modern" theater. In addition to an auditorium, the building housed a banquet hall in the basement, stores opening onto the street, and apartments on the upper floors. Sold in 1890, the building's name was changed successively to the Park Theater, the Waltham Theatre, the Scenic, and finally to the Waldorf Theater.

This photograph shows the lobby and the grand staircase of the Waldorf Theater during the 1920s. The theater closed on April 13, 1929, and a fire damaged the magnificent interior in 1932. After remodeling, the building now houses stores and offices.

The Embassy Theater opened in 1928 on Moody Street. Located in the Hall's Corner district of Moody Street, this new modern theater aimed to overshadow the other area movie houses. The Waldorf, the Maynard House, the Central Square Theater, and the James Opera House all operated in Waltham at the time. The Embassy closed its doors in 1969 and was the last of the big old-time theaters in Waltham.

The steamboat *White Swan* made its first trip up the Charles River in 1873 and operated as a pleasure cruiser from the Moody Street Bridge to Auburndale for 17 years. At the time of the *White Swan*'s launch, Waltham had two other steamers operating on the Charles River, the *Gosling* and the *Phoebe*.

Recreational activity in Waltham focused around the Charles River. Canoeists flocked to the waterway for their recreation and the demand for rental crafts exceeded the supply. Races among canoeists were extremely popular. In 1930, the Omicron Canoe Club sponsored an 8-mile race. Here spectators watch the event from the Moody Street Bridge.

Norumbega Park opened in 1897 as a rustic, open-air structure in Auburndale, Massachusetts. The park featured vaudeville, concerts, movies, and repertory companies. Waltham residents traveled to the neighboring town to visit the attraction using Charles P. Nutting's steam launch service from the Moody Street Bridge. Beginning in 1898, its 5¢ fare offered stiff competition to the land transportation running through Waltham.

The Charles River Carnival, held in September, indicated the formal closing of the boating season in Waltham. The main feature of the event was a boat procession with hundreds of vessels in line, dressed up with Chinese lanterns and other decorations. Judges awarded prizes to participants with the best displays.

The carnival took place every other year from 1885 to 1899. It was then held again in 1904, 1915, and 1930. It is believed that the *carte de visite* shown here is from the carnival of 1887. During this event, residents illuminated the boathouses, bridges, watch factory, and their backyards. A replica of one of Christopher Columbus's ships joined the parade and a man impersonated the famed "discoverer" of America.

Industrialist John Farnum acquired land north of the Davis and Farnum foundry for a horse track, which he named Central Park. Farnum was one of the first organizers of the New England Trotting Horse Breeder's Association. The park he created also served as an outdoor arena. The green in the center of the track showcased field days, circuses, baseball games, balloon ascensions, concerts, and other spectacles. In 1898, Buffalo Bill's Wild West show appeared here. Raytheon and Standard and Thompson now occupy this land along Grove Street.

Beginning in 1893 when the city secured the land, the 75 acres of Prospect Hill Park served as a playground for many Walthamites and out-of-towners. With its summit at approximately 482 feet above sea level, it offers scenic views of eastern New England. Skiing was once a favorite winter pastime on the hill. People picnicked there in the summer. The park is now being revitalized by the city.

In the 1870s, Prospect Hill served as a home to the "Hermit of Prospect Hill." Asa Fitz was a well-known writer of songbooks and associated with Horace Mann as an educational reformer. Later in life he erected a hut near the summit of the hill with the hope of adopting a simpler lifestyle.

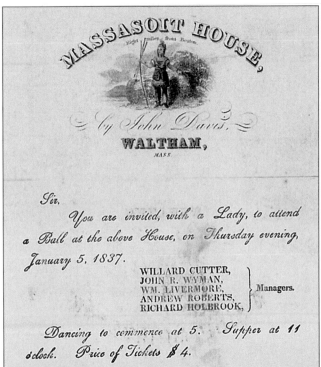

In 1836, the Massasoit House replaced the Cutting Tavern. Since 1742, the tavern stood near the present Ellison Road. Residents used this property to hold annual Thanksgiving shooting matches. After the Massasoit building burned in 1849, its land was divided and Linden Street was laid out to cut through the area.

The Beaver Brook reservation encompasses almost 59 acres of land bordering Belmont and Waltham. The property includes two ponds connected by Beaver Brook. This photograph, taken in the 1920s, shows the Waverley Oaks Duck Pond located where Waverly Oaks Road and Trapelo Road meet.

Beaver Brook rises in the town of Lexington and flows southward through Waltham and into the Charles River. The brook area is under the control of State Metropolitan Park Commission and comprises 34 acres. The first European travelers to Waltham in 1632 gave the brook its name when they encountered many beavers there, and it was around this locality that many of Waltham's early homes were built.

The 20 Waverley Oak trees near the Beaver Brook reservation inspired the name Waverley Oaks for this section of town. The trees are believed to be four hundred to nine hundred years old. James Russell Lowell wrote a poem about them and Winslow Homer painted them.

Opening night of Waltham's first Minature Golf League started at the Wal-Lex Recreation Center in 1961.

In 1947, George and John Rando collaborated with Frank Tortola and opened an indoor recreational facility known as Wal-Lex on a portion of the Randos' farmland. The facility housed one of the first automated bowling alleys in the world. A dairy bar, "kiddie land," and roller skating rink on the site also entertained people. In 1961, Waltham's first miniature golf league started at the recreational center.

The Doll Carriage Parade, photographed by E.M. Logan in 1949, took place on the Waltham Common as part of the annual Fourth of July celebration. Young Waltham girls proudly show their dolls to the photographer. In the background is the Waldorf Theater and Elm Street. Events on the Common continue today, most notably with the Mayor's Picnic in June.

94

Nine
Estates

In 1786, Christopher Gore purchased property in Waltham. In 1805, he built his grand manor shortly before becoming governor of Massachusetts. Historians recognize his mansion as one of the finest examples of early American architecture. The building and grounds have changed hands many times. In the property's unusual history, the Metz Automobile Company used it for offices and the Waltham Country Club set up a golf course there. In 1930, the Gore Place Society was established and purchased the estate to preserve it for posterity, opening the building to the public from April 15 to October 15 each year.

Many wealthy Waltham residents chose Beaver Street on which to build their estates. Home to the Clark, Warren, Lyman, Hammond, Sears, and Paine families, the street was one of Waltham's earliest and principal thoroughfares. The town's first meetinghouse stood here at the intersection of Lyman Street.

Theodore Lyman made his fortune in the fur trade and erected the family mansion, The Vale, on Beaver Street about 1796. The estate is home to the earliest greenhouses in the United States. To the south of the mansion ran Chester Brook, which the Lymans dammed to form three beautiful ponds. The waters offered great fishing to Waltham residents and reflected the beauty of the mansion.

Francis Cabot Lowell was famous as one of the founders of the Boston Manufacturing Company and for the town named after him following his death. This photograph shows his family and nurse enjoying the grounds of the Lowell Estate on River Street. The heirs of Francis Cabot Lowell later sold the 51-acre property to Oel Farnsworth, John R. Farnum, and Francis Buttrick for development. The mansion itself was converted to apartments.

General Nathaniel Prentiss Banks bought his estate in 1871. Built by Jacob Gale in 1798, the house stood in what is now known as Banks Square in the West End of Waltham. Massachusetts residents contributed to a fund set up to purchase the home for Banks upon his return from the Civil War. The estate originally comprised 40 acres, much of which Banks sold as house lots.

Annie Payson Call was an author and a teacher. She served as the principal of the Mount Prospect School for Boys, established by famous educational reformer Arthur Astor Carey. Constructed in May 1923, the purpose of the school on Worcester Lane was to bring poor Boston children together with wealthier peers. It was hoped that the privileged boys would positively influence the less fortunate ones. Located at 109 Worcester Lane and shown here, Payson Call's home was named Hillside.

The Hurricane of 1938 ravaged New England with an estimated death toll of 138 people. In the Waltham area there was much property damage. The Annie Payson Call Estate was among those that suffered. The estate comprised about 41 acres of woodland pines. Many of these trees fell during the storm, leaving the mess of debris shown in this photograph.

Jonathan Sanderson built the Sanderson House on Lexington Street around 1819. In 1824, the town bought the house and its property to use as a poor farm. Neighbors objected to this plan and the Piety Corner site was never used for that purpose. Lewis Bemis bought the property and carried on a shoemaking business there.

Rev. Samuel Ripley of the First Parish Church erected his parsonage on the site of the former Bird tavern and resided there for almost 30 years. Built in 1816, his home stood at 49 Pleasant Street. It is rumored that the house may have been used as a station on the Underground Railroad.

Built in 1818, the Daniel Emerson Homestead stood at the corner of Main and Lyman Streets. Emerson's blacksmith shop was across the street from the home shown here. Emerson was a nationally known wagon maker who produced items for the government during the Civil War. He is also said to have constructed prairie wagons for westward travelers. Emerson's house was demolished in 1951 to make way for a gas station.

Hamblin and Adelaide Hovey were wealthy benefactors who established a rest home, the Hovey Memorial building, and the Hovey House. Mr. Hovey served on the boards of many Waltham institutions. In 1923, Adelaide Hovey willed their estate, shown here, to construct the Parmenter Rest Home. In 1963, the house was razed to construct more modern elderly care facilities.

In 1854, the Warrens built their estate at 265 Beaver Street as a summer residence. Over 200 acres of forest and farmland surrounded the 18-room mansion. A working farm and farmhouse also stood on the property. Noted philanthropist Cornelia Warren inherited the estate from her parents and after her death it became the property of the Massachusetts Girl Scouts, Massachusetts Agricultural College, Harvard School of Landscape Architecture, and the City of Waltham. The mansion was razed due to lack of funds for upkeep.

In 1896, Cornelia Warren planted a maze replicating one at Hampton Court in England that dated from the 1690s. Miss Warren opened her labyrinth to the public so they could wind their way through a third of a mile of hedges to reach a little pond in the center. It was a great Waltham attraction, visited by dozens of people each day, but was removed because of the cost of upkeep.

In 1886, Rufus Lord built the house at 211 Hammond Street known as Lord's Castle. Sitting atop a high portion of land purchased from Oel Farnsworth, the home originally provided a view of many surrounding towns. Prominent in the construction business in Waltham in the late 19th and early 20th centuries, Lord is best remembered for his work on the Waltham armory at the corner of Sharon and Curtis Streets.

Sampson Reed, the founder of the New Jerusalem Church in Waltham, left land to the Boston Manufacturing Company, which the company split up and sold as house lots. In 1910, the Laightons purchased a lot on Bacon Street on which they built a home in 1914. It is one of the few examples in the city of Dutch Colonial revival architecture.

Robert Treat Paine Jr. was the grandson of Robert Treat Paine, one of the signers of the Declaration of Independence. The younger Paine married Lydia Williams Lyman of the Lyman family, who lived at The Vale mansion on Beaver Street in Waltham. With his engagement to her in 1860, Paine started visiting the city. In 1866, he erected his own mansion on Beaver Street, which was named Stonehurst.

In 1884, Paine hired the renowned architect Henry Hobson Richardson to design an addition to his house. Richardson moved the original building to a higher location on the property and surrounded it with the new construction. The resulting building contains the largest and only great domestic interior designed by Richardson still in existence. Frederick Law Olmsted, famous for his beautiful public gardens, designed the grounds of the private estate.

Noted architect Ida Annah Ryan built the Ryan home at 19 Boynton Street. The building was a wedding present for Ryan's nephew in 1914.

Located at 311 Beaver Street and built in 1785 by Jonathan Hammond, this house is one of the few late Georgian-style buildings in Waltham. Theodore Lyman purchased the property in 1815. In 1845, Charles Harrington bought the house and was instrumental in having the town set up Linden Street to run from his property to Main Street. In 1849, the building passed on to Cornelia Warren's grandparents and soon passed on to her father. Bentley College now owns it.

Ten
Farms and Open Areas

Originally an agricultural community, Waltham once encompassed many acres of open land and farmland. In 1738, Harvard College bought 160 acres of property lying to the southeast of Hardy Pond. This estate originally comprised three farms, which Anthony Caverley bought and brought together in 1728. Known as College Farm, this land was deeded to Nahum Hardy by Harvard in 1839.

Nahum Hardy made College Farm into a productive dairy facility. It is believed that he built this home on the Lexington Street portion of the property and sold about 100 acres and another home on the estate to his brother Noah.

Originally, Lexington Street formed a semi-circle from the First Church of Waltham in the east to Main Street in the southwest. The town soon straightened the route and extended it as a country road northbound to more remote areas. Waltham residents once knew Lexington Street as the "Road to Pond Meadow" or the "Road to College Farm." Heavily wooded, the road did not encourage early settlement, but residents soon realized that it had the most fertile land on which to establish farms.

About 1860, the Wellington homestead was the first residence erected on Lexington Street, and soon after John Viles developed the second residence on the street. The photographer viewed the Wellington farm, featured in this photograph, from Worcester Lane. Today, Totten Pond Road cuts through the old estate, running towards Route 128 and its industries.

Lexington Street boomed in the 1860s and William Childs established the Childs Brothers Farm at that time. He built a barn to accommodate the cattle that produced milk for his dairy. The barn also housed the horses that delivered the milk. In 1912, Childs built a new structure to accommodate the family's growing business. Constructed chiefly of wood, the building visible here sits in front of the old one.

Brown's Hill is located on Main Street near Lunda Street. Once referred to as "The Road by Deacon Brown's," the way was very rural. Looking west in the 1920s, one sees farmland.

In the 17th century, the trails that residents used to drive cattle to and from grazing became some of Waltham's first roads. Trapelo Road, Beaver Street, and Winter Street were among these ways. This photograph shows one of the farms on Winter Street, which runs to the west of Lexington Street between Totten Pond Road and Lincoln Street. Thomas Stratton was the first to build in this area.

Taken in 1902, this photograph shows the "Lane to Lake Street." Completed in 1877 by the town of Waltham to connect Lexington and Lincoln Streets, Lake Street runs by Hardy Pond. This pond has been associated with the following names: Great Pond in the Woods, Mead's Pond, Samuel's Pond, Sherman's Pond, Fisk's Pond, Smith's Pond, and finally Hardy's Pond. Before development of the Lakeview area, Lake Street offered open views of the pond nestled in the woods.

Albert Morse Ryan stands to the right in this photograph. His family gathers to his right at his home on Lexington Street. Ryan operated a milk business from his farm.

The northern part of Waltham remained rural into the 20th century, while most of the southern end was developing a city atmosphere. Many pig farms and dairies dotted the land along Lexington Street heading north. Taken in 1924, this photograph shows roadwork near Farnsworth's House and Piggery on Trapelo Road.

Living in this area as early as 1636, the Wellington family first settled near Trapelo Road. In the 19th century, the Wellington Estate included 90 acres of highlands and wooded areas with a pig farm and dairy on the estate. The Wellington Grove, shown here, was located near Hardy's Pond off Trapelo Road and was home to many birds and small wild animals. The Middlesex Sanitarium took some of the farm property by eminent domain in 1930.

Founded in 1848, the Massachusetts School for the Feebleminded relocated to Waltham in 1890. Renamed the Walter E. Fernald State School, the institution occupies 180 acres of land along Trapelo Road and Waverly Oaks Road. This northern section of Waltham is very hilly especially when compared with the flatlands near Main and Moody Streets.

In 1927, Massachusetts established the Metropolitan State Hospital at 475 Trapelo Road. Some of this land once belonged to Waltham residents, but also included areas in Belmont and Lexington. Set up as a "treatment center for the insane," the institution was among several hospitals located on the open lands of Trapelo Road. Its buildings were located on a hill and surrounded by wetlands and woods. The facility closed in 1992.

Theodore Storer descended from Robert Treat Paine. His home sat next to the Paine mansion and the two families often went horseback riding in the woods on the family grounds. In May 1973, the Storer family deeded their land, the Paine Estate, and the Storer home to the City of Waltham. Though the city destroyed the Storer house in 1975, the Paine mansion has been preserved along with walking trails for the public.

Joseph H. Curtis of Boston designed the Waltham Pumping Station, shown here. The city then built a new covered reservoir in 1906 and a new cement pumping station soon after. These sources were abandoned in 1949 when the city began taking water from the Metropolitan District Commission.

As the population of Waltham grew in the 20th century, housing developers quickly bought undeveloped areas near Main Street. In 1923, developers purchased the Bowker Estate to establish single-family dwellings in a district they called Warrendale. This area included 60 acres of land off lower Main and Warren Streets.

The almshouse was formerly a small residence owned by Samuel Garfield. In 1886, the need for larger accommodations prompted the city to develop the land shown here on South Street. They believed that use of this property for a poor farm "would in no way affect the future growth of the city." They did not consider its 17 acres valuable for residential development even though the land bordered the desirable South Side area.

East of Lexington Street, Trapelo Road farms were eased out by hospitals. West of Lexington Street, industry and highways pushed out the farms. This photograph taken by Aerial Photographs of New England in 1974 shows pig farms surrounding the Sylvania Systems Group property along Route 128. The City of Cambridge Reservoir also borders the highway.

Eleven
More Industry

In 1801, Nathan Upham started a papermaking business that he called the Upham Paper Mill. The business passed through many hands. John and Stephen Roberts bought it in the 1830s and renamed the plant the Roberts Paper Mill. Over its history, the mill saw many improvements in the process of paper manufacturing. In 1909, John's son William deeded the land to the city so that it could expand Mount Feake Cemetery.

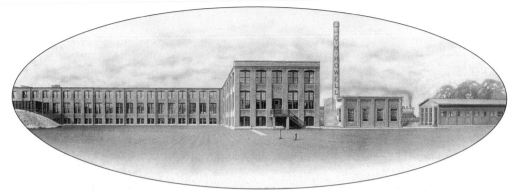

Originally establishing his business in Iowa, Charles M. Howell expanded the Howell Button Factory to Waltham in 1911. Located in the Bleachery District on Willow Street, the plant stood between the railroad and Foundry Avenue. Raytheon set up its Waltham base at this factory after the decline of the pearl button industry in 1933.

This aerial view shows the Waltham Bleachery and Dye Works and the Howell Button Factory on River Street around 1923. This bleachery was the first to finish cotton piece goods in one plant. Run by the owners of the Boston Manufacturing Company, the company gave its name to this southeastern section of Waltham known as the Bleachery District.

In the 1850s, Zenas Parmenter and his associates began a blackboard chalk-making business. They used a process invented by Waltham dentist Francis Field in the 1840s. The group bought Newton Chemical Company's old factory and named their business the Parmenter Crayon Company. In 1890, it combined with two Ohio crayon businesses to form the American Crayon Company, moving all production to the Midwest in 1902.

First established in Cambridge as the American Appliance Company in 1922, Raytheon Manufacturing Company moved to Newton in the late 1920s. Soon the business expanded to Waltham, acquiring the plant of the Howell Button Factory and later the factories of the Waltham Bleachery and Dye Works, the Metz Company, and the Davis and Farnum Foundry. A leader in the electronics industry, Raytheon was the first of many high-tech industries to locate in Waltham.

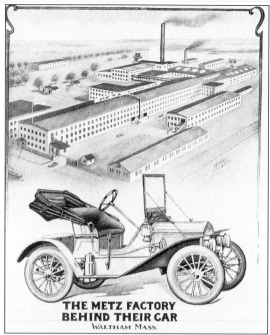

THE METZ FACTORY
BEHIND THEIR CAR
WALTHAM MASS.

Waltham was once a major center for the manufacture of automobiles. Charles Metz was president of the Metz Company, which incorporated in 1909. It became one of the most recognized names in the automobile industry at that time. In 1912, the company employed 1,500 people and produced 1,000 cars per month, but by 1923 it went out of business. Metz could not compete with Midwest manufacturers who found less expensive ways to build cars in the steel-producing region.

Standing in the lower left of this photograph taken in 1916, Charles Metz faces the camera. He built this factory located on River Street on the former property of Governor Christopher Gore. This plant supplemented an earlier Crescent Park facility. Metz used the mansion on the Gore estate as his home and as the manufacturing company's administrative offices.

Metz was always interested in airplanes and sponsored an aviation meet held on the Gore estate in 1911. Soon after, the company began building airplanes such as the one shown here. In 1914, they built a plant in Waltham for the production of airplane accessories to support the war effort.

METZ-AIR-CAR
BLERIOT TYPE

METZ COMPANY
Manufacturers of
Motor Cars and Aeroplanes

Before the Metz Company, Charles Metz incorporated the Waltham Manufacturing Company in Kittery, Maine, in 1893. He erected a factory for the business on Rumford Avenue in Waltham. The plant produced bicycles with low wheels and a light frame propelled by a chain. The business's greatest creation was the ten-rider Oriten, which served primarily as a promotional tool. This cycling wonder is now housed in Michigan at the Henry Ford Museum.

John Stark created watchmakers' tools, lathes, and other machinery for manufacturers. In 1870, Stark and his son moved their business to Moody Street. In 1887, John Stark Jr. continued the company when his father died. He erected the Stark building at what is now 416–424 Moody Street in 1891.

In 1853, the Waltham Gas Light Company incorporated; the first gas lines were laid the following year. The company began furnishing electricity for lighting a few years after Waltham became a city in 1884. In 1909, gas customers transferred to the Newton and Watertown Gas Company and Boston Edison purchased the electric business. Waltham Gas Light Company property at 684 Main Street was eventually sold to the Waltham Bag and Paper Company.

In 1902, William Henry Nichols set up his first machine shop in the basement of his home. In 1912, he erected his factory on Woerd Avenue. Inside the building, shown here on the right, workers constructed small machine parts and pumps. The plant produced much needed machinery for the government during World War I. To the left of the plant stands Nichols's home, from which he could supervise business operations until his death in 1951.

The W.H. Nichols Company continued after the death of its founder under the management of his sons. The business remained under Nichols family direction into the 1980s, when Parker Hannifin Corporation purchased it. Employees of the business in Waltham numbered between 250 and 834 over the years, depending on product demand. Nichols employees kick up their heels in this photograph.

121

The Judson L. Thompson Manufacturing Company produced buckles, rivets, and lacing hooks. Incorporated in 1890, the business settled on South Street in the Roberts section of Waltham. With offices and sales overseas in the 1940s, the Thompson Company was the largest manufacturer of rivets in the world. Similar to many other Waltham manufacturers, the company produced for the government during World War II. The company was sold in 1960 and later that decade Brandeis University purchased the property.

Edwin Land founded Polaroid Corporation in 1937. In 1955, the company expanded from Cambridge to Waltham on the former H.L. Stone Dairy site on upper Main Street along Route 128. By 1983, the company had five Waltham locations. It was once the largest employer in the city. The flight during which this aerial photograph was taken was furnished by Hopedale Aviation.

122

GTE developed through the merger of Sylvania Electric Products Inc. and General Telephone in 1959. It is one of the largest publicly held telecommunications companies in the world with revenues exceeding $21 billion. In 1955, Sylvania Systems Group was one of the first companies, along with Polaroid, to open in Waltham along Route 128. The company's headquarters in Waltham sits on the site of a former pig farm. This aerial view shows the company with the Boston skyline slightly out of view at the top of the photo.

Opening past Waltham in 1951, the new Route 128 attracted businesses from Boston by offering easy access to once remote locations. In 1952, Waltham rezoned to attract industrial developers trying to get away from the congestion of Boston. Built on former Waltham pig farms, the highway brought Polaroid, Cabot, Cabot and Forbes Realtors, and Sylvania Electronic Products Inc. within the first couple of years. Today, 3,500 businesses make Waltham their home. This photograph shows the opening celebration of Route 128 in Waltham.

Bibliography

Bacon, George F. *Waltham and Watertown: Their Representative Business Men and Points of Interest*. New York: Mercantile Publishing Company, 1893.

The Bleachery District of Waltham Past and Present: A Souvenir. Waltham: The Bleachery Old Timers, 1957.

Bolino, August C. *The Watchmakers of Massachusetts*. Washington, D.C.: Kensington Historical Press, 1987.

The Chronicle (newsletter of Chapel Hill-Chauncy Hall School) 14 (Fall 1987): 1–9.

City of Waltham Centennial 1884–1984 Special Edition of the News Tribune Waltham, Massachusetts June 21, 1984. Waltham: Waltham News Tribune, 1984.

Gitelman, Howard M. *Workingmen of Waltham: Mobility in American Urban Industrial Development 1850–1890*. Baltimore: The Johns Hopkins University Press, 1974.

Goldstein, Israel. *Brandeis University Chapter of Its Founding*. New York: Bloch Publishing Company, 1951.

Hall, Max. "The People's River: How Mankind Has Changed the Charles." *Harvard Magazine* (July-August 1984): 35–53.

Harrington, Elliott A. Letters to the *Waltham News Tribune*, N.D. Waltham Room, Waltham Public Library.

Hurd, Duane Hamilton. *History of Middlesex County: With Biographical Sketches of Many of Its Pioneers and Prominent Men*. Philadelphia: J.W. Lewis and Co., 1890.

League of Women Voters. *Looking at Waltham*, 1969.

Nelson, Charles A. *Waltham Past and Present and Its Industries*. Cambridge: Moses King, 1882.

Past and Present Waltham Progress and Prosperity (Watch City Souvenir). 1905.

Petersen, Kristen A. *Waltham Rediscovered: An Ethnic History of Waltham, Massachusetts*. Portsmouth, NH: Peter E. Randall Publisher, 1988.

Ripley, Samuel. *A Topographical and Historical Description of Waltham in the County of Middlesex*. Boston: John Eliot, 1815.

Sanderson, Edmund L. *Waltham As a Precinct of Watertown and As a Town 1630–1885*. Waltham, MA: Waltham Historical Society, Inc., 1936.

——. *Waltham Industries: A Collection of Sketches of Early Firms and Founders*. Waltham, MA: Waltham Historical Society, 1957.

——. *History of Piety Corner and Piety Corner Club and Its Antecedents*. Waltham, MA: Piety Corner Club, 1929.

Sanderson, Edmund L. and Elizabeth Castner. "History of the First Parish in Waltham 1696 to 1957." Waltham: First Parish Church, N.D.

Seventy-Fifth Anniversary of the Trinitarian Congregational Church of Waltham, MA. Waltham: Free Press Job Print, 1896.

Stone, Percival Mason. *Historical Articles on Waltham Published in the Waltham News Tribune*, 1948–1961 (typed manuscript and photocopied articles).

Swinton, John. *A Model Factory in a Model City: A Social Study*. New York: Brown, Green and Adams, New York, 1888.

Wacker, John and Assoc. Inc. *The Charles River, Waltham*. September 1974 study prepared for the Waltham Conservation Commission.

City of Waltham Annual Reports—various years.

Waltham Historical Society. "Publication No. 1." Waltham, MA: Waltham Historical Society Inc., 1919.

Waltham Historical Society. *Waltham Common*. (pub. no. 3). Waltham, MA: Waltham Historical Society Inc., 1926.

Waltham, Massachusetts. Its Advantages to Manufacturers and as a Place of Residence. Waltham: Waltham Board of Trade, 1887.

Index